LEARNING:
Reinforcement Theory

LEARNING:

RANDOM HOUSE STUDIES IN PSYCHOLOGY

Reinforcement Theory

SECOND EDITION

FRED S. KELLER

Emeritus Professor of Psychology, Columbia University

RANDOM HOUSE / NEW YORK

9 8 7 6 5 4

SECOND EDITION

Library of Congress Catalog Card Number: 74–81165

Manufactured in the United States of America

Preface to the Second Edition

Fifteen years ago, when Professor Hartley asked me to write an introduction to reinforcement theory that would serve for college freshmen, interested laymen, and those members of my own craft who might feel the need for a summary statement, I was frightened. Stripped of the usual accompaniment of curves and tables, lacking in experimental detail and scholarly documentation, and with little or no reference to historical foundations and debatable issues, would the account be worth reading? Would there be left enough of substance to engage the interest of such an audience, or of any other?

It now seems that these fears were ungrounded. The abbreviated account has apparently been useful at several educational levels and for a variety of readers. In this revision, I have tried to make it more so. Some new material has been included, especially in the area of *intermittent reinforcement,* and an appendix on *cumulative recording,* which has been an important feature of operant-behavior study since its earliest beginnings, has been added. Also, the Suggested Readings have been brought up to date.

Thousands of experiments have been performed since 1954 in the province of scientific theory and practice represented by this booklet, but little or no attention will be given to these studies here. The basic terms, the key conceptions, and the broad outline of the system have not been greatly altered, and *they* are still the concern of this introduction to learning from the standpoint of reinforcement theory.

F. S. K.
Kalamazoo, Michigan

Preface

It is very difficult to exaggerate the importance of the learning processes in the definition of human behavior. Students of Psychology have ever sought a proper understanding of this important field. Different theoretical "schools" have suggested different approaches, and integrated their concepts to provide for unified understandings of human behavior. Recent years, however, have seen an increasing number of systematic efforts to elaborate learning theory as the point of departure for understanding man—as compared, for example, with motivation, perception, biology, or society. One of the most stimulating of these approaches is that commonly identified as the *reinforcement* or *reward theory*.

In this paper, Professor Fred S. Keller provides a simple and brief introduction to the reinforcement theory of learning. Simple and brief though it is, all of the fundamental principles are identified, clarified, and their interrelationships and possible extensions indicated. It is, therefore, more than just the exposition of a theory of learning: it provides a learning-theory approach to all of Psychology. Though written simply, there has been no sacrifice of accuracy and scientific caution. This, then, is a document that will be appreciated not only by beginning students, but also by professionals who have found the customary expositions too technical or too bulky.

The writer of this paper has long been recognized as a theoretician, research worker, and teacher. He has contributed much to the development and application of reinforcement theory. In these pages he helps remove this approach from the esoteric—and makes it possible for an increasing corps of workers to understand, criticize, extend, and aid in the development of this important field of inquiry.

EUGENE L. HARTLEY
The City College, New York

Acknowledgments

The names of very few persons are mentioned in the pages that follow, but any psychologist-reader will quickly recognize my general indebtedness to Professor B. F. Skinner and his associates for the formulation of reinforcement theory here presented. He will also detect instances of specific indebtedness to researchers whose theoretical orientation came from the late Professor Clark L. Hull. He will even spot some old friends who are in no way connected with theory in any form. My reason for omitting personal reference is in each case the same. This is a booklet for the beginner. If he is aroused to go one step further in his study, he will soon make good the loss of names. If he is not, there will be no loss.

I am grateful to John V. Keller for a careful reading of this Paper at each stage of its writing; his comments were very helpful. Also, I wish to thank my colleagues, Ralph F. Hefferline and Wendell E. Jeffrey, for criticisms and corrections of the completed manuscript.

Anne S. Keller acted as subject in the experiment described in Section 4. Tardily, by about fifteen years, I express my gratitude for her cooperation!

FRED S. KELLER

Contents

LEARNING:
Reinforcement Theory

1 *Introduction*

Some form of the verb *to learn* is used in many situations. We learn, as babies, to tell one face from another, or a friendly voice from an angry one. We learn, perhaps, that screaming will sometimes get us things—and, later on, that it won't. We learn that some objects, if not properly handled, will cut, or burn, or pinch, or bruise our fingers. We learn to skate, to dance, to ski. We learn our table manners, our ways of speaking, and even our ways of showing emotion. We learn the multiplication table and we learn to recite Lincoln's Gettysburg address. We learn to fear the sound of the dentist's drill. We learn to tell the truth, and to be ashamed when we have told a lie. We learn the value of money, strength, age, title, rank, and position. And so on and on. The list is hardly begun, but maybe you can already see why it has been said that the field of learning is as large as the field of psychology itself!

Yet it is not easy to define learning. Consider for a moment, the cases just mentioned. Are all these learnings alike? Is learning to skate like learning to be ashamed? Or like learning the value of money? Like learning to ski? Is learning to fear the dentist's drill more like learning to avoid a flame than it is like learning to yell attention? Is there just one kind of learning? Are there two kinds? Seven? Or are there as many kinds as there are examples? What, exactly, *is* learning, anyhow?

These are difficult questions, and they are by no means the only ones that could be asked about learning. They cannot be answered in a word, a sentence, or even a book. We're still learning about learning, and the complete story will not be written for some time.

Meanwhile, it would be wrong to conclude that the situation is hopeless. Actually, it is just the opposite—more hopeful than ever before. Certain *general laws* or *principles* have recently emerged in the modern study of human nature. These laws or principles are not hard to understand and, if you grasp them firmly, they make a powerful tool with which to analyze all sorts of behavior. With their help, you should be able to bring into sharp focus almost any instance of learning that you are likely to meet in everyday life. And this includes all of the examples of learning mentioned above, no matter how complex they may seem to be.

2   *Operant and Respondent Behavior*

Before talking about principles, however, a line must be drawn between two kinds of behavior. One kind has been known, since long ago, as *voluntary* behavior, and the other has usually been called *reflex*. These two large classes of human activity together comprise just about all the examples of behavior in which a student of learning would be interested.

Voluntary and *reflex*, however, are bad words from a scientific point of view. The history of their use tells us that they have often meant different things to different people. In fact, there has been so much disagreement about the meaning of the two words that many psychologists have recently adopted the terms *operant* and *respondent* to replace them. It will pay us to follow their lead, hoping thus to avoid dispute about definitions. But you might note that, for some psychologists, *operant* and *respondent* come very close to meaning the same thing as their older counterparts, *voluntary* and *reflex*.

Respondent (reflex) behavior takes in all those responses of human beings, and many other organisms, that are *elicited* ("drawn out") by special stimulus changes in their environments. It is shown whenever the pupils of your eyes contract or dilate in response to changes in the lighting of a room; whenever your mouth waters at the taste of some choice bit of food; whenever a gust of cold air raises goose flesh on the surface of your skin; whenever you shed tears while peeling onions; whenever you gasp at an unexpected dash of water in your face; and in many other ways, some of which will be mentioned later on.

Operant (voluntary) behavior includes an even greater amount of human activity—from the wrigglings and squirmings and crowings of an infant in its crib to the highest perfection and complication of adult skills and reasoning power. It takes in all those movements of an organism that may at some time be said to *have an effect upon* or *do something to* his outside world. Operant behavior *operates* on this world, so to speak, either directly or indirectly. When you pick up a pencil, or when you merely ask someone to hand it to you; when you signal the bus-driver, or climb on the bus; when you make a telephone call; when you hum a tune, or glance at your watch, or work on a problem in mathematics—in these and in thousands of other everyday acts, you illustrate operant behavior.

Sometimes the effect of operant behavior upon the outside world is immediate and obvious, as when you kick a ball, open a door, or write a letter. Changes in the world may then be observed by anyone who will take the trouble to look for them. On other occasions, however, this is not the case. When you dial a telephone number but get no answer, or when you talk to yourself, aloud or silently, it isn't easy to see just how the environment is altered by what you have done. Only when you look into the history of such behavior will you find that, at some time or other, some form of the response in question really did make things happen. *Originally,* someone was aroused to action when you dialed the telephone number; and before you did any talking to yourself your speech must have had some effect upon the behavior of others or it would never have been acquired.

Respondent behavior, as already mentioned, is elicited automatically by special stimuli. A bright light, thrown into the dark-accustomed eye of a person with normal vision, will inevitably bring about a pupillary contraction. Operant behavior, however, is not quite so automatic, so inevitable, or so specific with respect to stimuli. Suppose you want a person to walk across a room, to raise his hand above his head, or to pick up a pencil from his desk. How would you elicit such responses? Would you employ a command, a request, or a plea? Would you try to put him through the desired act, using force if necessary? Would you make use of special lures or incentives? And would you feel as certain of the results of such stimulations as you would of the results of throwing light into someone's eye? And what if the person didn't understand your language; how then would you evoke the behavior?

The difference between operant and respondent behavior may be clearer if you think of their beginnings —the very first occasions on which they appear. Respondents, right from the start, are evoked by their own special stimuli. Food in the mouth will bring salivation, light in the eye will make the pupil contract, and so forth. The person has only to be born, you might say, in order for these stimuli to elicit their responses. In the case of operants, however, there are at the beginning no specific stimuli with which we can evoke them. Rather, we are compelled to wait until they appear before we can do anything about them. We simply do not know the specific stimuli that will cause an infant to make this or that distinct movement of the arm, leg, hand, or foot, or to vocalize for the first time in some specific way. It is for this reason that we may speak of operant behavior as *emitted* ("sent out") rather than elicited. Of course we know that operants do become attached to stimuli, and we shall see, in Section 12, how this attachment is achieved, but even then we shall be justified in arguing that operants and respondents are related to stimuli in very different ways.

3 *Respondent Conditioning*

Now we are ready to talk about principles. And, in connection with the first one, let's begin with some examples.

Case I: Suppose that, in a warm room, your right hand is immersed in a pitcher of ice water. Immediately the temperature of the hand will be lowered, due to a shrinkage or constriction of its blood vessels. This is an instance of respondent behavior. It will be accompanied by a similar, and more easily measured, change in the temperature of the *left* hand, where blood-vessel constriction will also be induced. Now, suppose that your right hand is dipped into the ice water a number of times, say at intervals of three or four minutes; and suppose further that an electric buzzer is heard briefly just before each dip. By the twentieth pairing of the buzzer sound with the cold water, the temperature change can be elicited *by the sound alone*—that is, without the moistening of either hand.

Case II: Now, imagine a person seated before a small moving-picture screen in a quiet room. On the screen, during a one-minute period, a printed word comes and goes at irregular intervals. During the same one-minute period, rolls of dental cotton, placed under the person's tongue, will soak up a certain amount of saliva, the exact amount being determined from the difference in weight of the dental cotton at the beginning and at the end of the minute. Then, in the same room, but with no dental cotton to hamper his eating, the same person is the guest at a series of short luncheons (of sandwiches, pretzels, and other titbits) during each one of which the word continues to come and go on the screen in front of him. Finally, with no food to eat, but with the cotton rolls in place again, the flashing word is presented for another one-minute test period and the salivation is measured as it was before. Result: the flashing word elicits much more salivary juice on the second test than it did on the first.

Case III: Think of still another human subject in a

laboratory room. This subject wears earphones and has electrodes attached to his left hand to permit the delivery of an electric shock. Other electrodes, attached to his chest and his left leg, are connected with a cardiograph to provide a record of heartbeats. When everything is ready, a tone of moderate pitch and loudness is sounded in the subject's ears for a one-second period. Six seconds later, a brisk electric shock is given to the hand. This combination of tone-followed-by-shock is repeated eleven times, at intervals of one to two minutes. By the eleventh pairing, the subject's heart rate will show a drop of fifteen to twenty beats per minute within a second or so after the tone is heard, and *before* the shock is felt.

These three cases are taken from actual experiments. Each one is a case of *learning*, just like that involved when you sweat at the sound of a dentist's drill or blush to tell a lie. Each one illustrates the same basic principle, known to you already, perhaps, by the name of "conditioned reflex." This principle was formulated in the early years of this century by the Russian physiologist Pavlov. It can be stated, a bit too simply, as follows: *If you pair a neutral stimulus with an eliciting stimulus a few times, this previously neutral stimulus will come to evoke the same sort of response*. The neutral stimulus, in our first case, was a buzzer; in the second case it was a printed word; and in the last case, a tone. Through pairings with ice water, food, and shock, respectively, they came to elicit, by themselves, the temperature drop, the salivary flow, and the change in rate of the heartbeat.

These conditionings occurred very quickly; only a few pairings were required in each case. This would not have been so if certain time factors had not been looked after and if certain precautions had not been taken. For instance, if the eliciting stimulus in each case had come *minutes* after, rather than seconds after, the neutral stimulus, conditioning might have been very slow. Or, if the neutral stimulus had *followed,* rather than preceded, the eliciting stimulus in each pairing, there might have been no conditioning at all. Moreover, the speed of conditioning would also be affected by the number of distractions present, the kind of instructions given to the subjects, the intensity of the stimuli employed, the physiological state of the subject at the time of the experiment, and so on. You can see that there is more to conditioning than can be told in a one-sentence statement.

Our definition is inadequate in another respect. The buzzer, the flashing word, and the tone in our three examples were "neutral" only in a relative sense—only in that they did not, to begin with, have the *same* effect on behavior as their partners, the ice water, the food, and the electric shock. Each of them probably had *some* effect on behavior before the pairing, some subtle influence that you might not even be able to observe. Each, you might say, had its own reflex response; each was really eliciting in its own right. Consider the following simple diagram, where *S* refers to *stimulus* and *R* to *response:*

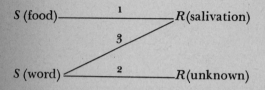

Probably we ought to say that, in conditioning, two *reflexes,* two stimulus-response connections, were paired, rather than two stimuli. Conditioning requires the formation of a *third* reflex, composed of the "neutral" stimulus and the response to the "eliciting" stimulus.

Pavlov recognized all this. The third reflex was his *conditioned* reflex, and he spoke of the two reflexes upon which it was based as "unconditioned." In the same way, he spoke of conditioned and unconditioned *stimuli*. Food was called the unconditioned stimulus for a dog's salivation; and the stimulus (a tone) with which it was paired became the *conditioned* stimulus for the same response. (And we ought to add, of course, that the tone was an unconditioned stimulus for some other response—for example, some startle effect—before any conditioning began.)

Another term of Pavlov's has come to be very important in modern psychology. In describing the effect of food in conditioning a dog to salivate at the sound of a bell, he referred to it as "reinforcing." The food reinforced the connection between the neutral stimulus and the salivation. This is like the effect of the ice water and the electric shock in our Cases I and III. Today, we have extended the meaning of the term somewhat, using "reinforcement" also as the rough equivalent of the "reward" or "punishment" of operant behavior.

Pavlov's principle, as he formulated it, applied especially to glandular activity, and he worked mostly with the salivary glands. But it applies as well to "smooth muscle" activity, of the sort involved when the pupil of your eye dilates, your blood vessels contract, or the hair rises on your skin. All of these are *reflex* or *respondent* changes. In addition to these, Pavlov felt that his law applied to "motor" or "striped muscle" activities—movements of the head, arms, legs, fingers, and so on. Today, however, we take a more conservative view. We think that the law deals not with operants, but with respondents exclusively. One modern theorist has gone so far as to say that it applies mainly to emotional reactions and is therefore dependent on the workings of the autonomic nervous system. This may or may not be the whole story, but at least you can see why the word *respondent* was included in the title for this section.

4   *Operant Conditioning*

In taking up the next principle, an example is again appropriate. This time our subject is a little girl, about seventeen months old, and the experimental situation is an ordinary living-room, modified slightly to serve a laboratory purpose. Our observations begin as the little girl runs into the living-room from the hallway and attempts to engage the attention of her mother, who sits by the window reading. Failing in her efforts, the child turns away. As her eyes wander over the room, they suddenly alight upon a new feature. Through a narrow gap between the sliding doors to the dining-room, a small, T-shaped handle projects itself. Just beneath the handle is a tin dish, easily within the child's reach. Approaching these objects quickly, but warily, the child touches the handle with her finger, and looks into the dish. As she does so, a small pellet of chocolate drops into the dish from a tube the other end of which is out of sight in the dining-room. Startled by this, the little girl momentarily withdraws from the dish, but returns to pick up the pellet and eat it. A few seconds later, she grasps the bar firmly and pulls it downward an inch or so, causing a second pellet to be discharged into the dish. From this time on, with rapidly growing efficiency, she operates this lever mechanism, eating each pellet as it comes, until the chocolate finally loses its appeal.

In this simple case, a powerful principle of behavior is illustrated. Edward L. Thorndike, a great American psychologist of this century, called it the *Law of Effect,* and conducted many experiments to show its importance in human and animal behavior. In essence, this law states that *an act may be altered in its strength by its consequences.* The *act,* in our example, was that of lever-pressing; the *strengthening* of this act was seen in its increased frequency of appearance; and the *consequence* of the act, of course, was the pellet of chocolate that dropped into the tray.

Well known among Thorndike's own studies are those in which hungry cats were given access to bits of food whenever they manipulated the appropriate latch, lever, or other device that opened the door of a "puzzle box" within which they were imprisoned. Progress of the cats in this task was measured by the decrease in time required for them to get to food on successive occasions of confinement. Thus, as a cat solved his problem, the number of seconds he needed to operate the escape device was gradually lessened until his performance approached perfection.

Today we commonly speak of such "effect learning" as *operant* or "instrumental" conditioning, and often measure its strength in terms of rate—the frequency with which it occurs in time when the organism (animal or human) is free to respond at will. In the case of

our little girl, we would have expected a response to
the lever now and then, even in the absence of special
reward. But, when chocolate followed closely upon
lever-pressing, the likelihood of repeated response was
immediately increased—the rate was suddenly raised.
As the child continued to procure pellets, of course,
satiation took place and the lever-pressing rate fell off.
You would make no mistake in assuming, however,
that, when her hunger for chocolate returned, her
lever-pressing behavior in this situation would be quick
to reappear.

This operant conditioning may be pictured as follows:

$$R \rightarrow S$$

R is the response (lever-pressing); $\rightarrow$ means "leads to";
and S is the reinforcing stimulus, the chocolate. There
is no need, at this point, to talk about the stimuli that
might, or might not, have led to the pressing of the
lever. As mentioned earlier, they would have been very
hard to identify at the time when the response was first
made, and we might have been hard put to *elicit* the
pressing. Later on, however, you are going to see that
the R in our diagram does come to be related to environmental cues, and we are going to examine the conditions under which the relation is established.

5 *Positive and Negative Reinforcers*

Chocolate is obviously not the only kind of reinforcing stimulus that could be used to condition such an operant response as bar-pressing. Actually, it is but one member of a large family of reinforcers—a family of so-called "positive" reinforcers. This family includes all those stimuli that, when *presented*, act to *strengthen* the behavior that they follow. Under appropriate states of need, many other foods (or drinks), perhaps even certain lights or tones, would have increased the rate of lever-pressing in the same way that the chocolate did in our example.

But this isn't all. There are negative, as well as positive, reinforcers that may be used to condition operant behavior. Some stimuli strengthen responses through their *removal*. We don't ordinarily use these stimuli in experiments with children, or even with adults, but there are many examples of the way they work in non-experimental situations, and in experiments on lower animals. When a boy removes his shoes because they pinch or are filled with pebbles; when he takes off his jacket because he is too warm, or puts it on because he's cold; when he closes his eyes or covers his ears to cut out glaring lights or piercing sounds—in all these cases, he is reinforced by *getting rid of* stimulation. Similarly, white rats, in laboratory studies, have often been trained to run, jump, push on a panel, step on a pedal, depress a lever, or perform some other act, when their only reward is an escape from annoying doses of electric shock or other intense stimulation.

One may say, then, that a negatively reinforcing stimulus is one that strengthens the response that takes it away. But it is also a stimulus that *weakens* the response that *produces* it. Suppose, for example, that our child had received, for every lever-pressing, an electric shock rather than a chocolate pellet. Under such conditions you can guess what would have happened. The rate of lever-pressing would have been drastically affected. It would have dropped well below the level of its unconditioned occurrence—that is, the frequency with which it would naturally have occurred in the absence of any special effect. At least this is the conclusion one would reach on the basis of common sense or of those animal studies in which operant responses have been followed by intense stimulation. Quite generally it has been shown that strong shocks, bright lights, loud sounds, and so forth, will effectively *suppress* all the behavior that has brought them on. The suppression may not last, especially if the organism is left in the same situation after the negative reinforcement has been discontinued, but its existence is not to be doubted. (We return to this problem in Section 10.)

6 *Extinction*

Psychologists are often asked how to get rid of already-conditioned behavior, how to *un*learn, or how to learn *not* to do something. This is a question that leads in many directions; and there is much more to the answer than can be given here. But the basic formula is simple enough: *the way to unlearn an already-conditioned response is through "extinction"—through the withholding of reinforcement.*

Consider the Pavlovian conditioned reflex. It is *set up* by following a conditioned, "neutral" stimulus with an unconditioned, reinforcing one. It may be *broken down* by presenting the conditioned stimulus, but withholding the unconditioned. Recall the examples of respondent conditioning given earlier. A temperature drop was conditioned to the sound of a buzzer; a salivary secretion was conditioned to the sight of a flashing word; and a change in heart rate was conditioned to a one-second tone. All this has been described. The fact was not mentioned, however, that, later in each experiment, the conditioned response was extinguished. In the first case, the buzzer was repeatedly sounded, but the hand was *not* dipped in water; in the second, the word flashed again and again, but *no* food accompanied it; and, in the last case, a succession of tones was *not* followed by electric shocks. The result, in each case, was the same. The strength of the conditioned response declined, until the effect of the pairings was lost and the conditioned stimulus again became "neutral."

These are instances of respondent extinction, but the same fundamental rule holds for the operant as well. If reinforcement is withheld, the response will ultimately return to its original unconditioned rate (sometimes called its *operant level*). In some experiments, as in the case of the little girl who received chocolate for lever-pressing, the removal of reinforcement is the cause of considerable emotion. Excessively vigorous and rapid responding, even angry attacks upon the reward device that no longer works, may alternate for a while with periods of operant depression and sulkiness. The number of responses in each volley gradually decreases and the periods of nonresponse grow longer and longer. Finally, the strength fades to the level of an occasional apathetic reaction, and the extinction is just about complete.

Extinction, for both operants and respondents, is sometimes very slow to take place. In a few cases, investigators have reported that it didn't occur at all. This is rather disturbing. It suggests that some of our conditionings may stay with us longer than we wish—that we might be burdened, perhaps for life, with anxieties, compulsions, and obsessions that are by no means easy to carry. Will I always have this fear of dogs, or of speaking in public? Will I never be able to break myself of smoking cigarettes? Will this haunting tune or painful thought never go away?

Things are probably not as bad as this, however. For example, the alleged failure to get extinction of a conditioned pupillary contraction, a conditioned salivary secretion, or some other conditioned respondent, may have a different explanation. We know that *operant* behavior may sometimes produce *unconditioned respondent* effects. This has often been referred to as the *voluntary* control of *involuntary* action. Thus, by tensing certain muscles one may provide the unconditioned stimuli for a change in pulse rate, blood-vessel constriction, and so on. It may well be that such operant control of respondent behavior, established at the same time that the respondent was being conditioned, can be maintained after the conditioned stimulus for the respondent has ceased to have any effect. In other words, before we can be absolutely certain that a conditioned respondent will not extinguish, we must be sure that our subject has not discovered, unknown to us or even to himself, his own special operant for producing the same effect on an unconditioned basis— that is, by giving himself the stimulation that will elicit the same respondent change.

Conditioned *operants,* too, may resist extinction, sometimes to a fantastic degree, so that, to all appearances, they may be inextinguishable. Animal experiments portray this most vividly. A pigeon, for example, may be conditioned to peck at a small disc or key on the wall of an experimental chamber. When, after long training, extinction is begun, the pigeon may respond as many as 7,500 times during the first hour, without any sign of let-up. In two more hours, he may emit nearly as many responses again, and extinction will be incomplete. Watching the bird, you might say that he was incurably addicted to key-pecking; you would wonder that he did not stop from sheer exhaustion! Ultimately, of course, he will no longer respond to the key, even when refreshed and still very hungry for the food that his pecking once produced, but an impatient observer might easily go away with the opinion that the habit was unbreakable.

7 *Intermittent Reinforcement*

A prime agent in generating a great resistance to extinction in cases like that just mentioned is the *sched-*

ule of reinforcement that has previously been in effect. When a pigeon is rewarded *intermittently,* rather than on every occasion of a pecking response, a highly machine-like form of behavior will develop after long-continued training. If the reinforcements come at regular *intervals of time,* say every five minutes, short periods of nonresponse will alternate regularly with longer periods in which the bird quickly accelerates to a rate of two or three times per second and continues at this speed until the next reinforcement occurs. The bird appears to "tell time." He never responds directly after eating (he has never been reinforced for responding *then*), but is busily pecking again by the time the next reinforcement is due.

Laboratory workers speak of the above schedule as one of *fixed-interval* reinforcement, since a fixed amount of time must pass between reinforcements. However, if the reinforcements depend on the bird's making the same *number of responses* on each occasion, a somewhat similar alternation of rates will appear. When reinforcement comes, the bird eats his grain, waits a bit, and then taps out the required number of responses, say twenty, at a steady, rapid clip. This is known as a *fixed-ratio* schedule, in this case a ratio of twenty-to-one—twenty responses to one reinforcement. (We do not talk of a "time discrimination" here, since we know that the bird gains nothing by pausing after he has eaten.)

A different picture of response rate emerges when the pigeon's reinforcements come in random, haphazard fashion, either at variable intervals or after a variable number of responses—that is, on a *variable-interval* or a *variable-ratio* schedule. A single, regular rate of responding then takes over, interrupted only when the bird takes a few seconds out for eating. This rate may be high or low, depending on the type of schedule (variable-ratio typically produces higher rates than variable-interval schedules) and on the average time that elapses between reinforcements. When rewards come close together, the pecks may come at a rate of three or four per second; when they are far apart, the rate may be three or four *per minute*. Such rates may be maintained for long hours of each day and for weeks on end.

The effects of these different schedules of intermittent reinforcement can be seen, as noted at the beginning of this section, in the amount of responding that will occur when reinforcement is completely discontinued—when extinction goes into effect. After a procedure of *continuous* reinforcement, when every response has been rewarded, extinction can be expected to cut down the response rate very soon and with clear signs of emotional upset, as described in Section 6. *Intermittent* reinforcement provides in all cases for a greater resistance to extinction, with far less emotional involvement. The organism may respond, hour after hour, in the same steady unruffled manner as was shown during training. This is especially evident when the rewards have previously come at uneven intervals of time, in which they were sometimes given in close succession and sometimes far apart. Rate of responding, under such a schedule, may be indistinguishable from the rate that is maintained during the first few hours of extinction.

A consideration of the effect of different reinforcement schedules upon later, nonreinforced, responding leads to the conclusion that an important factor in accounting for resistance to extinction is the similarity of the training conditions to the extinction conditions. When reinforcement has been given regularly for each response during training, the change to conditions of nonreinforcement is drastic. But when the organism (rat, bird, or human being) has become accustomed to going for long spells without a reinforcement, the conditions, at least for awhile, are exactly the same as the training conditions. Unless the organism can tell the difference between the two, responding will continue at the same rate as before. And, if such a conclusion is warranted, operant behavior must be thought of as more closely tied to environmental stimuli than has previously been suggested in these pages. This is an important point, and one to which we shall return in later sections.

8   *Superstitious Behavior*

In all the schedules of reinforcement described in Section 7, the experimental subject, a pigeon, had to peck a key before he could get his grain; the reinforcement, we say, was *contingent upon* a specific kind of response. This is, perhaps, a normal state of affairs in our lives, as well as in experiments with pigeons; we usually have to *do* something in order to *get* something. But not always. Sometimes we seem to be paid for doing *nothing*. What effect, if any, does reinforcement have upon us then?

Consider another pigeon study. The bird is again hungry and in his experimental quarters, where he has had a chance to eat grain from a tray on earlier occasions. There is *no* particular response that he is now supposed to emit, or which has been conditioned, but, at regular fifteen-second intervals, a tray-full of grain will be automatically presented for a five-second period of eating. Will his behavior be recognizably affected by this *noncontingent* reinforcement?

The answer is *Yes*. In a very short time, under these conditions, the bird will develop some special form of response. He may walk around in circles within the experimental space; he may shift back and forth from one foot to the other; he may extend his head repeatedly toward some part of his chamber; he may "bow and scrape" again and again, or make pecking movements toward the floor. Any one of these, or other, actions may appear with a frequency like that of pecking a key, although it never really produces the grain. The response appears to have been "caught" by the reinforcement that happened to follow when it was first emitted. Before it had time to extinguish, another reinforcement came; and soon a full-blown "superstition" was established, not unlike the behavior of a gambler who talks to his dice or walks around the table to change his luck.

Noncontingent reinforcement must be frequent at the outset, in order to get results like this. Otherwise the accidentally reinforced response will extinguish sufficiently to be replaced by another that, in turn, may be replaced by still another, destroying the ritualistic effect. If one begins, however, with closely spaced reinforcements, the superstitious behavior develops quickly. When firmly established, the interval may then be increased gradually without causing a shift in behavior. Also, if the time between reinforcements is always the same, a time discrimination will develop, just as in the case of a pecking response on a fixed-interval schedule. Finally, the superstitious response may be hard to get rid of. One bird hopped from side to side more than 10,000 times before reaching a point of near extinction.

9 *Low-Rate Responding:*
An Example

Psychologists have sometimes attempted to control the rate of responding in other ways than those described above. *High* rates have been set up by reinforcing responses only when they follow one another very closely, and *low* rates have been attained by reinforcing responses only when they are far apart, when the "inter-response times" are no shorter than a certain number of seconds or minutes. A homely example may be of some interest.

Our subject, a small boy, is seated at a table in his home, with a microphone in front of him and a small tin cup at his right. Behind him stands the experimenter, with a handful of pennies and a stop-watch. He has just instructed the boy to "say words" into the microphone, at whatever speed he wishes, or with whatever amount of repetition, but avoiding sentences or other meaningful sequences. To these instructions, the experimenter adds: "Now and then, while you're doing this, I'll drop a penny into the cup. When the experiment is over, you can have all the pennies you have earned. All you have to do is say words."

After some hesitation, the words begin to come:

microphone, tree, grass, table, dinner, wallpaper . . . names of objects in the room or outside, and words of more personal reference. One of the words, *flowers,* is picked at random by the experimenter as the occasion for a penny. Immediately it is said again, and again it is reinforced, until five pennies have been earned in quick succession. The boy's response is conditioned, and the control of rate can now be attempted. From now on, *flowers* will be reinforced *only when it comes ten seconds or more after it was last uttered.*

The word undergoes some extinction at first, fading in force and spoken with less assurance as it slows down to a stop. Then, after a series of other words have been emitted, it reappears and, since ten seconds have elapsed, is reinforced again. Within a few minutes of training, a good time discrimination is developed and most of the *flowers* responses are reinforced. (If one occurs too soon, of course, the experimenter simply sets his watch back to zero so that another ten-second-or-more delay is required before the next response will be successful.)

One result of this little study may come as a surprise. Between each utterance of the word, *flowers,* the boy did not remain silent, as he might well have done. Instead, he filled the ten-second period with other words, and these words did not occur entirely at random. Instead, as practice continued, a fairly regular *sequence* of such words developed—a kind of "superstitious chain." Immediately after receiving a penny these words were not predictable, but, as the time for the next reinforcement approached, the same ones always appeared in order: *ship, sea, beautiful, red, flowers.* Here we seem to have another case of *noncontingent* reinforcement, since only the *last* response in the chain was required in order to earn the reward.

But there is more. The boy in this experiment made an excellent "time discrimination." He seldom responded, after reinforcement, in less than ten seconds, and seldom did he over-shoot by more than two or three seconds. Yet he had no idea that time was involved in the experiment! He "thought" he had to learn a series of responses, and, when the experiment was over, he apologized for his lack of success, saying: "I'm sorry, but I couldn't figure out all of the words you wanted me to say." Such results raise interesting questions concerning the part played by our own behavior when we are discriminating "time." Did the superstitious chain of responses hinder the boy, or help him, in his unconscious timing? More generally, when we tell time without a clock, to what do we respond?

This experiment could lead us in two further directions. We could discuss similar but more formal studies of what is technically known as the *differentiation of low-rate responding* (*drl*, for short), with animals, children, and college students as experimental subjects. Or we could move directly to the topic of stimulus-response *chaining*. The first alternative would quickly take us into more specialization than ought to be attempted in a primer like this and the second will be better understood after we have paved the way more fully. So, let us simply change the subject now by turning to a question, or at least an aspect of a question, that has puzzled mankind from earliest days—the question of *punishment* and its effect.

10 *Extinction and Negative Reinforcement*

If you were asked to suggest ways of hastening the
extinction of a strongly conditioned operant, it is a
safe bet that, sooner or later, you would come up with
the proposal that *punishment* should do the job. You
would probably mean by punishment something like
a shock, a slap, a blow, or some other negative reinforcer that could be applied to the unwanted response
whenever it occurred. If the lever-pressing of the little
girl in Section 4 had been rewarded for many days,
intermittently, and with many things besides chocolate, and if you were now intent upon extinguishing
the response as soon as you possibly could, wouldn't
you suggest cutting the process short with something
like a mild shock or a rapping of the knuckles?
Wouldn't this be psychologically sound? Wasn't it
said, on page 16 of this paper, that the child's behavior
would have been weakened by shocking every response
to the lever that she made? And were not negative
reinforcers defined in part as stimuli that weaken the
responses that they follow?

The question of the effectiveness of "physical" or
"corporal" punishment is an old one and it cannot be
disposed of with a simple Yes-or-No answer. It is undoubtedly true that a good strong negative reinforcer
will put a stop to almost any kind of operant behavior
that you can name; but this does not tell the whole

story. Many a parent has discovered for himself the value of a "good spanking" in bringing a child's chronic misbehavior to an end; yet not every parent has felt entirely secure about the possible after-effects.

For obvious reasons, there are few, if any, experimental studies of the effect of severe punishment upon human reactions. In recent years, however, a good-sized body of fact has been accumulated from animal research. The upshot of this research may be briefly noted here. First, it is well established, as noted above, that the effect of a strong shock or other negative reinforcer upon an operant like lever-pressing is to decrease its frequency of occurrence. This is true if the stimulus is applied during regular positive reinforcement, during intermittent positive reinforcement, during extinction, or before any conditioning of the operant has taken place. Moreover, within limits, the stronger the punishment the greater the effect upon the operant rate.

Secondly, if the punished animal is left in the punishing situation for a long enough period of time under either of these conditions, but without the shock or other punishing agent, he will recover from the effects. The recovery will apparently be quicker when the punished response continues to receive positive reinforcement, either regularly or intermittently, than it will be under extinction conditions or in a relatively "neutral" situation. In one animal study, wherein white rats were punished with shock during the first ten minutes of extinction of the lever-pressing response, the effect of the punishment disappeared almost entirely during one hour in which the subjects were confined in the situation *with the lever absent*. As much time, and nearly as many responses, were subsequently required before the lever-pressing was extinguished; and the rats behaved almost exactly like animals that had never been shocked at all.

Thirdly, it appears that the emotional responses associated with the punishing stimulus are conditioned in a respondent fashion. When a shock, for example, is presented in a special place, say in an experimental chamber of some sort, the place itself becomes a conditioned stimulus capable of producing the same effects as the shock did. And with these respondent changes there goes the depression of whatever operant behavior was in progress. The place, you might say, comes to excite fear, and the fear puts a stop to other things— for example, lever-pressing. The extinction of the fear, like any respondent extinction, requires the withholding of the unconditioned, reinforcing stimulus (the shock). As this extinction goes on, and the place loses its fearsome aspect, the operant response begins to reappear. The animal returns to whatever reinforced or nonreinforced activity prevailed before the shock was given. If intermittent positive reinforcement is still in effect, he goes back to his previous rate; if extinction conditions are still present, he takes up his unreinforced responding once more. The punishment may have set him back in his responding, but it will not have permanently altered his operant rate or hastened the process of operant extinction.

This transient effect of punishment is to be expected only if the punishing stimuli are no longer applied and only if the subject is kept in the punishment situation for a long enough period of time—that is, until the effect of the conditioned emotional stimuli has had a chance to extinguish. If, however, the animal, after being punished, is given an opportunity to escape to a different environment, in which no further hurt is received and all his needs are satisfied, then the effect of

punishment may not appear to be so transient. The
outcome of punishment will then be *avoidance,* a topic
with which we shall deal in Section 16.

11   *Generalization*

Some cases of "learning" do not clearly qualify as such.
They represent, instead, the reappearance of behavior
that has already been well strengthened under the
same, or nearly the same, conditions. Consider the case
of a chimpanzee who has learned to use a long bamboo
pole for raking in fruit from outside his cage. He has
now been given two shorter poles, which he holds in
his hands. Neither will reach the fruit, but they may be
telescoped, like the links of a fishing rod, to do so.
Suppose that, in manipulating the two poles, he brings
the solid end of the thinner one into close visual relation with the tubular end of the thicker one. Being no
amateur at poking sticks into holes, he may quickly
insert the one end within the other. Then, finding himself in possession of a single long pole, he may turn, in
a flash, to rake in his food. There may take place in all
this a small amount of operant conditioning. The ape
may come to the point more quickly on the next test.
But the outstanding feature of his solution of the
problem is the reinstatement of two acts that had form-
erly been conditioned in the presence of similar stimulation.

Such reinstatements of previously conditioned re-

sponses were treated by Thorndike, some years ago, as
examples of "response by analogy," a basic law of behavior. He stated the law simply: "To any new situation man responds as he would to some situation like it,
or like some element of it." Pavlov, thinking exclusively of reflex behavior, and of dogs rather than
human beings, came independently to a similar law,
but called it *generalization*. Today, we use Pavlov's
term, rather than Thorndike's, but we apply it to
operants as well as respondents, and we recognize, more
than did either of these men, its theoretical importance.

An example of generalization from Pavlov's laboratory may be helpful here. A dog was conditioned to
salivate at the sound of a 1000-cycle tone. When the
response had been well established to this tone (the
only one used during training), a number of other
tones were tested for their effect upon the dog's
salivation. Without exception, they elicited the response, although to a lesser degree than had the original tone. The stimuli "generalized." That is, the dog
responded to all of them in the same way, except in
the *amount* of saliva secreted. Tones that were near in
frequency to the conditioned stimulus produced, in
general, more salivary flow than tones that were further
away on the frequency scale.

So, we may say that when an operant or a respondent
has been conditioned in one stimulus situation, it may
then be evoked, without further conditioning, in
another stimulus situation. To this we add that the
power of the new stimuli to evoke the response will
depend upon the physical features that the situations
have in common. Going still further, we may say that
there are various *scales* or *continua* along which these
stimuli may generalize. Tones, for example, will generalize along a scale of sound-vibration frequency

(pitch), a scale of energy (loudness), and possibly others. Comparable continua exist in sight, touch, and the other senses.

In everyday life, examples of generalization are so common that they go unnoticed. They are most obvious, perhaps, in children, where they are often amusing. Parents smile at the child who calls out "Doggie!" at the sight of a horse, a cow, or some other four-legged creature; or they may laugh to hear a child say that soda-water "tastes like my foot's asleep." They may fail to realize that the same principle is involved when the responses are much more common and undramatic. They may not see that one child's "Chickie!" in response to a robin is essentially the same as another child's "Birdie!" The simple fact is this: a child, or an adult, who has been conditioned to respond in a certain way in a certain situation will still respond in this way when each element of the situation has been altered along one or more of our basic continua, and even when some of the original elements of the situation are lacking.

There is another side to this picture that may be noted briefly to prepare you for the discussion in the next section. Generalization may take place during extinction as well as during conditioning. An example from the study of respondent extinction will show how this happens. Suppose that the galvanic skin response (a change in the electrical resistance of the skin) has been conditioned to a vibratory stimulus applied at each of four points on a person's body—the calf of the leg, the thigh, the side, and the shoulder. Now suppose that, later, extinction is partially achieved at *one* of the four places, say by stimulating the calf alone with the vibrator until the conditioned skin reaction has been greatly reduced in amount. If, at this stage of the experiment, you then test the effect of the vibrator at the remaining spots, you will find that the response has been weakened at each of them, with the least effect at the greatest distance from the calf. Ultimately, of course, none of the spots will produce a conditioned effect when stimulated, and you might say that the "generalization of extinction" is then complete.

12 *Discrimination*

By now it must have become pretty apparent to you that operant, as well as respondent, behavior gets tied to stimuli very early in an individual's life. You may even have wondered if it did not get tied to *too many* stimuli. If generalization operates in the manner just described, why shouldn't a person go through life responding in the same way to *all* visual stimuli, in another way to *all* sound stimuli, and so forth? Shouldn't every visual stimulus generalize in some degree with every other visual stimulus? And shouldn't this be equally true for all the other senses?

We know, of course, that this doesn't happen. The question is foolish. Yet, how is it that people make distinctions between things that they do? Why are we able to distinguish, not only between dogs and other quadrupeds, but between several breeds of dog? And why can a dog-fancier recognize many more differences than we can?

Such questions as these may be answered simply, by

stating the principle of *discrimination: Connections between stimuli and responses that have come about by way of generalization may be separately broken down.* Or, to put it in another way, reinforcement may still be given to the original connection, while all the *derived* connections are permitted to undergo extinction. Ultimately, the response will be made exclusively, or almost exclusively, to the original stimulus; and, correspondingly, the generalized stimuli will be without effect.

Recall the little girl whose lever-pressing produced chocolate candy. When this response was well conditioned, the child would undoubtedly have continued to respond to the bar in spite of rather gross modifications in the stimulus situation. Sizable changes in room illumination, in the visual background of the bar and tray, or in the appearance of the bar itself would not have disrupted her behavior appreciably. That is, there would have been considerable stimulus generalization. But, if bar-pressing had been reinforced *only* when the room illumination was high, *only* when the visual background was of a certain pattern, or *only* when the bar was of a certain size, color, or brightness, then a discrimination would have been formed: the response would have extinguished in all but a very restricted set of stimulus conditions.

The respondent case is similar. The dog, in Pavlov's laboratory, conditioned to salivate when a 1000-cycle tone is sounded, will also salivate, because of generalization, to tones of other frequencies. But, if these other tones are presented again and again without being followed by food, and if reinforcement continues to accompany the 1000-cycle tone, the time will come when they no longer elicit salivation, although the 1000-cycle tone continues to do so.

This is an oversimplified account of the discriminative process, and objections to it may have suggested themselves to you. For example, what about the generalization of extinction that was mentioned in the last section? In the case of Pavlov's dog, why doesn't the nonreinforcement connected with other than the 1000-cycle tone weaken the response to the 1000-cycle tone itself? The answer is that it does, but that the 1000-cycle tone doesn't lose as much power to elicit the response as the other tones do. Every reinforcement associated with the 1000-cycle tone more than makes up for the generalized loss. Moreover, every gain in power of the generalized tones to excite the response (through reinforcement of the 1000-cycle tone) is more than cancelled by the direct effect of extinction upon these tones. Gradually, by little additions and subtractions, the two conditions of stimulation pull apart from each other and the discrimination is established.

This process has been demonstrated again and again with animals, but far less often with human beings, especially adults. An important reason may be that most human beings, before reaching the psychologist's laboratory, have a long and complicated history of discriminative function. It is not often that we can really start from scratch in breaking down generalization. The stimulus discriminations of daily life have usually taken their toll well in advance of our experimental procedures. Some improvement may still be possible; we may still bring about a slight upward shift in the percentage of responses that get reinforced. But we are seldom able to narrow down greatly the range of stimulus values that will produce a given response.

We may, of course, still test the subject's final capacity to discriminate. We may determine, for example, just how small a difference can exist between stimuli before there is no more than a fifty-fifty chance of a correct response. This has been for many years the concern of the branch of psychology called *psychophysics,* which takes as its principal sphere of activity the study of adult human sensitivity to stimulus differences. Occasionally, too, it has been the concern of those who study animal and child behavior—sometimes with surprising results. In a now-famous experiment, Pavlov once trained a dog to discriminate visually between a circle and an ellipse. Then, step by step, he brought the ellipse closer and closer to the shape of the circle. Ultimately the discrimination broke down, as you would expect. With continued demands upon his powers, the dog finally became "neurotic," to the degree that he had to be removed from the experiment and given a long rest for the sake of his health. Similarly, in another Russian experiment, a six-year-old child was compelled to distinguish successively between metronome beats of 144 per minute and beats of 92, 108, 120, and 132 per minute. No trouble arose in discriminating 144 from 92 or 108 beats per minute; the distinction was made readily, in very few trials. But trouble began when 144 was compared with 120 beats per minute; and when the final discrimination between 144 and 132 beats per minute was attempted, the child became seriously upset, showing extreme rudeness, disobedience, excitement, and aggressive behavior, as well as sleepiness in the experimental situation.

There's a great deal more that might be included here about discrimination. Whole books have been written on the topic, usually under the heading of "sensation" or "perception." From a scientific point of view, this topic is perhaps the most advanced of any topic in psychology. Our main object at the present time, however, is to understand "learning," and you can see by now that discrimination plays a pretty important part in that story. Thousands, perhaps hundreds of thousands, of discriminations must be made by each of us in meeting the requirements of the world about us. Operant behavior, for which we could find no eliciting stimulus at the start, later comes to be almost completely under the control of stimuli. And it does so merely because we *give* reinforcement in the presence of one stimulus and *withhold* it in the presence of another.

You may remember that, in Section 3 on Respondent Conditioning, and again in Section 4 on Operant Conditioning, a simple diagram was presented to help make these principles clear. Let's now see what sort of picture we can use to represent discrimination. You know in advance, of course, that nothing very new will be involved. Generalization we have seen to be merely a kind of bonus derived from *conditioning,* and discrimination (the breakdown of generalization) is largely a matter of *extinction.*

When we take up the case of *respondent* discrimination, we run into trouble right off. Because *any* conditioning of a respondent requires some degree of discrimination. For example, the first effect of pairing a 1000-cycle tone with food for a dog as he stands in his harness within an experimental chamber is to condition salivation to tone *plus* stimulation from the harness itself *plus* the other sights and sounds and smells within the room. We do not reinforce, however, in the presence of all these stimuli *unless* the tone is present too. So, very soon the response is extinguished in the absence of the tone, but appears when the tone is part of the compound—and this is *discrimination.* Later on, of course, we may go further. We may reinforce in connection with one tone and extinguish in connection with others, in the manner already described. A diagram to indicate this further step might look like this:

In this case, S^D (ess-dee) represents the stimulus (e.g., the 1000-cycle tone) that has been selected from among other tones for reinforcement. S^Δ (ess-delta) represents a tone that is *not* followed by food and which therefore loses its connection with the response.

Similarly, we might represent an *operant* discrimination as follows:

$$S^\Delta$$
$$S^D \underline{\hspace{4cm}} R \longrightarrow S$$
$$S^\Delta$$

In this diagram, the S^D indicates the stimulus to which the operant has now become attached, and the S^Δ's indicate the generalized stimuli that have lost their power to evoke the response. Hence they have no connection with the R of the diagram.

(In talking about these two cases, the word "cue" is often used as a synonym for S^D or "discriminative stimulus," especially when operants are involved. It would be time-saving to have another short word for use with respondents, to show when the conditioned stimulus has been discriminated, but no good one has yet turned up.)

One more point. The above-mentioned procedure of discrimination (reinforcement under S^D and extinction under S^Δ) is sometimes treated as a special case of *reinforcement schedule*, a so-called *multiple* schedule. A discrimination could be shown, not merely by responding in the presence of one stimulus and not responding in the presence of another, but by different patterns of response rate under the two (or more) stimulus conditions. Stimulus A, for example, could be present when a fixed-interval schedule of reinforcement was in effect; stimulus B could be present during fixed-ratio; and stimulus C could be present during variable-ratio. Before long, the organism would respond under each different stimulus condition with the pattern of response appropriate to the particular reinforcement schedule that was in effect at that time.

13 *Differentiation (Shaping)*

In dealing with the principles of operant and respondent conditioning, of extinction, and of discrimination, we have, in a sense, dealt with several kinds of learning. Extinction, when considered by itself, might seem to be more a matter of unlearning, but we have seen that it is vital to discrimination, which no one would hesitate to call learning, of a very important kind. If, now, you will look back at the examples given on page 3 of this paper, you will see that we have covered a good part of the territory that we set out to explore. But you will also see that we haven't covered it all. The present section should add considerably to your ability to handle those examples, and the sections that follow will add still more.

The word *differentiation* is not a very good one for our present purposes, since it is often used as if it meant *discrimination*, which it doesn't, at least in this account. *Skill* would be a better word if it weren't so inclusive, taking in both discrimination *and* differentiation, and perhaps something more. *Shaping* is the term most commonly used, but it too raises problems since it is sometimes taken to mean a change in the *stimulus control* of some responses (for which a better term would be *shifting*). In this account, we'll stick to *differentiation* and try to make its meaning so clear that it won't be confused with anything else.

Let's begin with an example. Imagine a laboratory room in which the principal piece of equipment is a pin-ball machine, one of those amusement devices in which a plunger is drawn back and released to send a steel ball on an inclined run where it may make contact with certain up-rights or fall into certain holes to provide a performance score. *This* pin-ball machine, however, is a special one. A shield hides the course of the ball from the operator and keeps him from seeing how far back he pulls the plunger before each release. Another shield keeps him from seeing two "kymograph drums" on which are recorded (1) the rate of his plunger-pulling, and (2) the distance of each pull. Nor can he see the 15-step scale lying parallel with the shaft of the plunger and making possible fifteen electrical connections that control the appearance of a little red light through a window at his end of the machine. (Each step on this scale is separated from the next by 2.8 millimeters, a bit less than an eighth of an inch, and it can be arranged so that a pull of the plunger to a point between any pair of these steps—for example, between steps 2 and 5 or between 10 and 13—will cause the red light to come on when the ball reaches the end of its course.) The only thing known to our operator, a college student, is that he is to take part in a "study of nonvisual skill," and that he will see a red light flash in the little window when his response has been correct.

The subject's first task, after being introduced to the situation, is to pull the plunger of the machine for five minutes. We tell him to use a rate and a force of pull that seems natural or comfortable. He obliges us and responds at a rate of about twenty-two pulls per minute, or a little oftener than once every three seconds. The average distance of his pull (our measure of the force of his response) is about 32 millimeters, a little more than an inch, but some of the pulls are more than this and some are less. There is, in other words, some degree of variability in his response, even when working with an optimal rate and force.

When this level has been determined, we tell our subject that the light will now be available, and we set the switches so that only a pull to a position between points 2 and 5 on our scale will lead to a flash of the red light. This gives him a range of 8.4 millimeters within which his responses will be correct. We let him work at this until he secures twenty reinforcements, a goal that he reaches quite easily, in thirty-one pulls. Then, without his knowledge, the switch-setting is shifted from 2–5 to 10–13. The range is exactly the same as before, but the setting is farther along on the scale. He requires 179 pulls, more than five times the earlier number, to obtain his twenty lights. Thus, it appears that mastery of the first setting stood in the way of mastery of the second. With repeated shifts, however, between 2–5 and 10–13, the subject improves in his speed of readjustment. When one setting fails to work, he shifts more and more readily to the other. Nonreinforcement, after a run of reinforcements, becomes a cue for trying something different.

In the next stage of our experiment, the subject begins responding with a switch-setting of 2–6. After twenty reinforcements have been obtained, we change the setting, without his knowledge, to 3–6 decreasing the range by 2.8 millimeters. He does as well at this setting as he did before, so again we raise the requirement, this time to 4–6. When twenty lights have again been secured, we change it once more, to 5–6. The number of responses required to get twenty reinforcements at the 3–6 setting is 32; the number required at the 4–6 setting is 47; and the number at the 5–6 setting is 93. That is, the number of responses increases as the subject's range of movement is more and more restricted.

Finally, our subject is given further sessions at the 2–5 switch-setting under different schedules of reinforcement: (1) *regular,* in which each response is reinforced if it meets the correct distance requirement; and (2) *intermittent,* in which (in this case) there is no reinforcement until 10 correct responses have been made. After each session, reinforcement is stopped entirely and a count is made of the number of responses made before the subject shifts to a new level of force. Result: our subject, as you might expect, shifts more readily after a period of regular reinforcement than after a period of intermittent reinforcement —in fact, about four times as readily.

This experiment is only a small part of one in which there were fourteen subjects and several additional procedures, but it is enough of a sample with which to begin our discussion. Some of the main features of differentiation are clearly to be found within it. There is, for example, an initial *variability* of response, without which differentiation could never take place. It was obvious in the preliminary five minutes of "natural" pulling, but it was also present at the beginning of the subject's testing at the 2–5 level of switch-setting. The variability was mainly apparent in the *distance* of plunger pull, but it also occurred in connection with *rate,* and it might have been found in the *duration* of the pull, had such been measured. We could even have discovered differences in the *form* or "topography" of the response—the way the subject grasped the knob of the plunger on successive pulls— but this would have been difficult to measure.

Secondly, there is a *selective reinforcement* of response. When the red light follows upon responses that range in force between points 2 and 5 or 10 and 13 of the scale, rather than the original 1 and 15, the subject soon makes a successful adjustment. His range of forces narrows down abruptly and, when the experimenter changes the "rules," he is able to shift quite readily from one range to another. If the range becomes too narrow, his accuracy drops off (if we carried this too far, "neurotic" behavior might develop); and his speed of shifting will depend upon the number of shifts already made, as well as the reinforcement schedule; but no one could doubt that his behavior is shaped by the presence or absence of the light that follows each response. Plunger-pulls that get no light fall off in frequency; those that bring it on become more numerous.

Thirdly, when the experimenter reduced the range of successful responses from a wide to a narrow band, moving by small steps from a setting of 2–6 to one of 5–6, he illustrated the importance, in the shaping process, of *successive approximations* to the desired behavior. Had he jumped abruptly from the broad band to the narrow one, from the "easy" to the "hard," he would have greatly increased the errors and time required for his subjects to solve their problem. By selectively reinforcing small advances in the right direction, he reduced the chances of failure and reached his goal without undue delay.

Through such approximations, at the simplest level, laboratory rats may be taught to lift heavy weights, walk on their hind legs, show a fast reaction time, and so forth; children may be trained most efficiently in writing, speaking, and many other basic functions, even to exercise "self-control"; and experts in every field of art and skill may be led to the peak of their perfection. In every case, the teacher follows the same rule. He begins with variability in the behavior of his pupil; he reinforces change in one direction and extinguishes it in another; and he assures maximal success and minimal failure by successively approximating the behavior he desires.

Finally, the change in our subject's behavior *does not depend on changes in his external world*. There are no outside cues to tell him when reinforcement is available and when it is not, or just what force he will have to use in order to get it. Such a connection could be set up, as you will soon see; but the only discriminative cue employed in the purest type of differentiation comes from the movement itself, rather than from any external source. The subject will tell you, after he has practiced awhile, that he can "feel" when his response is going to be successful, but this "feel" comes from the contractions of his own muscles as they begin the act.

It is not a stimulus over which the *experimenter* has any direct control.

Our experimental example is but one of many that could have been chosen. Studies of dart-throwing, line-drawing, ball-tossing, and the like abound in the literature of experimental psychology, along with studies of movement in various practical situations. Many of these are cases of pure differentiation. Also, there are scores of everyday skills that are based upon the same process. The golfer who sends the ball from the tee with his driver, the basketball player who shoots a basket, the quoit-thrower, the archer, the bowler—these are but a few of our activities that may be perfected in unchanging stimulus situations. Less striking, but actually more important, are the differentiations involved in the mastery of such universal skills as walking, talking, writing, singing, and dancing.

The basic process, in all these cases, may be pictured, not quite correctly, in this way:

$$\begin{array}{l} R^\Delta \\ R^D \longrightarrow S \\ R^\Delta \end{array}$$

Here, the R^D represents that variant of the response which leads to reinforcement, and the R^Δ (*R*-delta) indicates a variant which did *not* receive reinforcement. The R^D and R^Δ thus correspond to the S^D and S^Δ in our diagram of discrimination.

The diagram is inadequate because, like the one representing operant conditioning (page 14), it implies that our stimulus environment plays no part whatever in dictating our response. It would lead one to think that lever-pressing had nothing to do with the presence or absence of a lever in the situation, that the basketball played didn't need a basket, or the archer a target. The truth of the matter is that the processes of discrimination and differentiation march together, hand in hand, from the very beginnings of our behavioral development. At one time, discrimination may take the lead; at another time, differentiation. When a child reaches for a ball, he gives evidence that the ball is a discriminative stimulus, but his improvement in accuracy with repeated reachings is mainly a matter of differentiation. The change in the response occurs in *the presence of* the cue all right, but it doesn't depend upon any *change* in it.

By the time we are adults, every one of us has acquired an enormous number of differentiated responses that may be made to an even larger number of discriminative cues. In addition, everyone has the ability to change smoothly and rapidly from one response to another in the face of an ever-shifting stimulus field. You can see this vividly as you watch the participants in such sports as boxing, tennis, and hockey, in which a lightning speed of movement is required to keep pace with the stimulus variation produced by the movements of an opponent. But you can see it also, if you look, in practically every sphere of human conduct, indoors or outdoors, verbal or nonverbal, at play or at work. The musician who follows his printed score, the radio operator who copies Morse code, the stenographer who takes dictation or types from her shorthand symbols, the factory worker at the assembly line—in these instances and many others, the process may be seen.

No visual arrangement of lines and letters can hope to picture the rapid interplay of stimulus and response involved in the cases just cited, but the following diagram may still be of some slight aid in portraying the simplest combination of discriminative cue and differentiated operant. It takes us at least one small

$$
\begin{array}{ll}
S^\triangle & R^\triangle \\
S^D \text{————————} R^D \text{————} S \\
S^\triangle & R^\triangle
\end{array}
$$

step further in our project of building a unified picture of what goes loosely by the name of "learning" in our daily lives.

14 *Chaining*

Seventy-five years ago, if you had asked a teacher of the new science of psychology to talk to you about the nature of "learning," he would have told you nothing about conditioning, extinction, generalization, discrimination, differentiation or reinforcement. Pavlov, who gave us all these terms in their technical sense, was at that time busily examining the digestive activity of dogs and was still eleven years away from the Nobel Prize he received for so doing. Thorndike was only nineteen years old, with at least three years to go before engaging in the puzzle-box studies that were to lead to his famous Law of Effect.

Instead of such topics and such developments, you would have heard a great deal from your psychologist about the "association of ideas" and the "laws" governing such associations, particularly as described by eminent British philosophers of the eighteenth and nineteenth centuries. You might also have listened to an account of some long and painstaking German experiments on "memory" and "forgetting"—experiments in which subjects were required to master series of "nonsense syllables" (*mib, gop, ruz, ved,* etc.) under very special conditions. At most you would have been treated exclusively to an account of such matters as now fall within the province of a single chapter in the field of learning.

Interest in "serial learning," both verbal and non-verbal, was heightened at the turn of the century, when studies of animal behavior began to feature the running of mazes by white rats, and when certain influential physiologists began to describe the "successive compounding" of reflexes in animals as low in the evolutionary scale as the frog and the earthworm. By 1914, John B. Watson, the founder of early "behaviorism" in American psychology, had combined his knowledge of these developments with his understanding of Pavlov's principle, to argue that the learning of nonsense syllables and maze pathways was no more than the formation of "chains" of conditioned reflexes.

Today we think that Watson was wrong in several of his assertions about this kind of learning. We feel sure, for example, that syllable-connections and correct turns in a maze are not instances of *respondent* conditioning. We agree, however, that Watson was basically sound in his attempt to account for such habit-formations by referring to more fundamental things. We see, too, that these fundamental things are differentiation, discrimination, and generalization, which depend, in turn, on conditioning and extinction.

We express this notion of chaining, today, in the simple statement that *one response may produce the stimulus for the next.* And we recognize, perhaps more

than ever before, that it is the exceptional case in which
responses do *not* occur in chains. It is seldom that a
single response or stimulus-response connection does
not lead to another or arise from something that has
gone before.

The essential state of affairs in chaining may be
outlined well enough by doubling the diagram that
was discussed in the last section.

$$S\triangle \qquad\qquad R\triangle \quad S\triangle \qquad\qquad\qquad R\triangle$$
$$S^D \text{———————} R^D \rightarrow S^D \text{———————} R^D \rightarrow S$$
$$S\triangle \qquad\qquad R\triangle \quad S\triangle \qquad\qquad\qquad R\triangle$$

Here it is seen that a discriminative stimulus may evoke
a differentiated response that will in turn produce the
discriminative stimulus for another differentiated response that leads, in turn, to reinforcement.

Let's take, as our example of chaining, not the
learning of a maze or a series of nonsense syllables, but
the behavior of a white rat named Pliny, from the
University of Minnesota! * Pliny did nothing that a
raccoon, a monkey, or a child could not have done as
well or better, but the very fact that he was a rat, and
not as complicated or varied in his ways as these
others, will help to illuminate the chaining process in
its bare essentials.

Pliny's accomplishment amounted to this. He would
first pull a string that hung from the top of his cage.
This pull would cause a marble to be released from an
overhead rack. When the marble fell to the floor, he
would pick it up in his forepaws and carry it across the
cage to a small tube that projected vertically two inches
above the floor. He would then lift the marble to the
top of the tube and drop it inside, whereupon a pellet

* A pictorial account of this animal's achievement appeared in
Life, May 31, 1937.

of food was automatically discharged into a nearby tray. Pliny would then approach the tray, seize the pellet, eat it, and turn again to repeat the sequence of acts. In this way, he earned his living, day after day.

Here, then, is a chain of operants, each induced by its own specific cue. (Respondents are less commonly seen in chains and will not be treated here.) Visual or tactual stimulation from the string and its surroundings probably set off the string-pulling response. String-pulling brought into action a new set of stimuli, provided by the marbles as it arrived. These made up the cue for the grasping and carrying responses that put the animal in the presence of another visual compound, the tube. The lifting and letting-go responses that permitted the marble to drop into the tube produced, in turn, the sound of the food-magazine which led to tray-approach and, finally, stimulation from the food itself. With completion of the eating behavior, the entire sequence began again.

Exactly how many distinct responses there were in Pliny's well-perfected chain is a question, so smoothly did each blend with the next. It is pretty certain, however, that there were more to begin with than there were later on. For example, the animal had considerable trouble at the start in letting the marble go after he had raised it into position above the tube opening. Lifting was clearly one response, letting-go another, and it was hard for him to time the two properly. His behavior was like that of children when learning to throw a ball: they either let it go too soon or hold on to it too long. Later in his training, however, Pliny's timing was so good and the elements were so well joined that you would not have known when one response left off and the other began. As in the case of many human actions, and especially human speech, units originally quite distinct group themselves into larger units, reducing notably the number of perceptibly different links in the chain.

It is also hard to specify the cues that were active in controlling Pliny's final chain. It is very likely that the number decreased with practice—that Pliny came to respond to mere fragments of the earlier array. Other experiments have indicated that such a narrowing-down may occur. But, in the absence of special tests, we are in no position to say which element of the stimulus situation at any stage of the sequence was the one to touch off the response.

Pliny's chain, unlike those involved in most human studies, required a large amount of training in differentiation for several of the links. The responses employed in carrying, lifting, and dropping the marble, although probably shaped in part through past experience in handling food, still had to be given a lot of attention. The rat's trainer had to watch carefully, and to reinforce selectively, all those little changes in each response that pointed toward improvement. As with all delicate differentiations, he had to avoid shifting too rapidly from one stage of advance to the next, seeing to it that ground was steadily gained but that extinction had no chance to occur when a new demand was made. If the differentiations had already been formed—if the basic skills had already been established, the chaining itself would have been no great problem for the animal. Each separate act would have been easily added to the others, in the same way that human beings link together old, well-differentiated words in the memorizing of a poem. Before such a differentiation had been made, however, we might compare Pliny to a person, unacquainted with Chinese, who is asked to react to a succession of written characters in that language by pronouncing each one correctly the moment it occurs!

Down through the years, many questions have been asked about serial learning. Most of them have been questions about the mastery of strings of nonsense syllables. It has been asked, for example, how the speed of such learning is related to the *number* of items in the list to be learned. Or to the *kind* of items in the list—for example, the degree of their similarity to real words or parts of words. Or to the *place* of the items in the list—that is, whether one part of a list is learned more readily than another. Or to the previous mastery of other lists, having the same or different item content. These are a few of the problems that have been raised. Each has been the subject of much investigation, discussion, and theorizing. But only in fairly recent times has John Watson's lead been seriously followed and an attempt been made to relate them to the basic principles of conditioning, extinction, discrimination, and so on. This attempt has nevertheless been, in the main, quite fruitful, and it may be worth your while to consider a few examples of it.

Take the matter of number of items in the list to be memorized. Nonsense-syllable experiments indicate that a remarkably large number can be strung together. As many as 300 were mastered in one investigation, and the limit was probably not yet reached! It appears, however, that the amount of time that has to be spent on each syllable increases appreciably as the number of syllables goes up. It may take a minute and a half, on the average, to memorize 12 syllables, but require 195 minutes to master 300 syllables, which is only 25 times as many syllables as 12.

An important factor in accounting for this increase in difficulty may be the similarity of the syllables involved. As one learns to recite a list like *jid, fap, tev, wof, pes, yut, zoy,* and so on, each uttered syllable provides a large part of the cue for the utterance of the next. Sooner or later, as the number of syllables increases, one runs out of differences between cues. Every new syllable resembles one or more already in the list. That is to say, it *generalizes* with it. This may happen even when the subject groups the syllables into larger compounds like *fap-tev* or *wof-pes,* or when he supplements the syllables in some way, as by changing *wof-pes* into something more like *wolf-pest.*

Generalization may also play a part in explaining the trouble we have in mastering a long series of *numbers.* Only ten digits, 0 through 9, are available for use in such series, and if it weren't for common groupings, like 1492, 5280, 31416, and 1776, together with various personal ones (telephone numbers, license numbers, etc.), we would have more trouble with these than we have with nonsense syllables. Grouping may save the day for a while, but eventually we run out of differences between groups. At last the time comes when no addition can be made without a corresponding loss. We get to be like the college president, also an ichthyologist, who complained that every time he memorized the name of another student he forgot the name of a fish!

Animal studies tell a similar story of generalization as a limiting factor in the setting-up of chains. Maze-learning experiments, with white rats as subjects, show that the mastery of the correct path from entrance to exit depends mainly upon cues provided at the successive turns where choices must be made. The differences between these cues may be reduced in a couple of ways. Critically important sense-organs (for example, the eyes) may be eliminated surgically; or, each unit of the apparatus may be made as much like each other unit as possible. In either case, the result is the same. The animal's speed of learning is diminished, and so is his final level of achievement.

A special case, in which the amount of generalization is extreme, is that of the "temporal" maze. In this device, rats are trained to pass through the *same* point of choice on, say, four successive occasions, turning left on the first two, and right thereafter. The shift from left turns to right ones on the third choice in this maze is the source of most of this trouble. There is no change in the external cues to tell them that they must now go to the right instead of the left; and there is so little difference in their ways of responding on the first and second runs that they cannot easily pick up any cues from their own behavior—as they might if they were permitted to make four distinctly different responses on their runs through the choice point. So delicate is the discrimination that few rats ever succeed in developing the left-left-right-right sequence.

This is barely an introduction to the problem of chaining. A full account would include a treatment of the famous "association experiment," sometimes used in lie-detection and in psychotherapy, and in which the subject responds to one word with another as quickly as he can. It would deal with the question of unseen, or *covert*, chains or links of chains that figure so prominently in the analysis of "meaning," "thinking," and "perceiving." It would comprise a discussion of dozens of concepts and scores of experiments; and it would bring up many points of high debate. It would provide you with a large body of facts; and it might even stir you to think of new methods or to devise new researches in this field. But not all these things can be covered here. For present purposes, it will be enough if you have understood clearly the basic principle and seen how it relates to those discussed in the earlier sections of this book. In a moment you will see that it is also related to one in the section to follow.

15 *Secondary Positive Reinforcement*

Some stimuli are *naturally* reinforcing, either in a positive or a negative way. Food, for a hungry organism, has a kind of "inborn capacity" to strengthen behavior. So has drink, under conditions of thirst. Similarly, electric shock and other intense forms of stimulation work, right from the start, to depress behavior (or strengthen the behavior that removes them). These, we say, are *primary* reinforcers.

On the other hand, it is pretty apparent that such stimuli make up but a small part of all the things that reinforce. In fact, we rarely see conditionings, especially at the human level, in which food, drink, or electric shock plays any part. Much more often, it would seem, responses are strengthened or weakened by the approval or disapproval of other persons, by praise or blame, by promises or threats, by "Right!" or "Wrong!" And these are events that must have *acquired* their reinforcing power. We call them *secondary* or, sometimes, *conditioned* reinforcers.

The way in which secondary reinforcers acquire their power was suggested by Pavlov in the early years of this century. He pointed out that, when a conditioned reflex is well established in a dog, it may then be used as the basis of a second conditioning. Thus, if a metronome beat had been made into a conditioned stimulus for the salivary response, it might then be paired with another "neutral" stimulus, say a black square, in forming a "second-order" conditioned reflex. That is, the metronome beat *alone* would serve as the reinforcing stimulus for the new conditioning, and it would do this because of its previous association with the primary unconditioned stimulus, food. Pavlov did not, however, carry the concept of secondary reinforcement very far. It is only in recent years that we have come to recognize its tremendous importance and have understood how operant behavior comes under its control.

Let us, then, examine the way in which this happens —how secondary reinforcement is related to *discrimination,* how it helps in the making of *chains,* and what significance it has in everyday human affairs. And, since psychology, like biology, is democratic in its attitude toward species differences, why not begin with a sample of chimpanzee behavior?

Our subject is a male, about six years old. His name is Moos, and he lives in a small colony of apes at an anthropoid research station, where he has been a participant in psychological experiments for most of a two-year period. In the present experiment, he is one of six animals, all younger and less sophisticated than he, and, with them, he has already been through several stages of training. *First,* he was taught to insert poker chips into the slot of a vending machine. White chips were employed, and the insertion of one chip was followed immediately by the delivery of a single grape into the food-tray of the machine. Because of his history as an experimental subject, Moos was rapidly led to do this. Only once did the experimenter have to demonstrate the process. Directly thereafter, Moos picked up a chip from the floor and clumsily inserted it into the slot. A few more trials increased his skill appreciably. That is, his response was readily differentiated in the direction of quick, smooth, effortless procurement of his reward. *Secondly,* he, along with his companions, was trained to make a discrimination between white chips and brass ones. In this training, he was regularly presented with two kinds of chips in pairs on a board that he could reach from within his restraining cage. If he seized the white chip (S^D) for use in the vending machine, a grape was delivered; but if he chose the brass one (S^Δ) and put it into the slot, no grape appeared. Moos solved this problem in four sessions of 20 choices each, during which he made a total of 10 errors—that is, 10 responses to S^Δ.

Now, a new piece of apparatus is brought into Moos's cage. This is a work-machine. Its essential features are (1) a lever and (2) a poker-chip holder. Movement of one end of the lever upwards through an arc of 90 degrees brings the poker-chip holder within easy reach of the operator. With the machine in position, and with Moos attentive, the experimenter places a white poker chip conspicuously in the holder and then steps aside. The chimpanzee then approaches the machine and begins to shake and tug at it vigorously, until the experimenter interrupts him for a brief period. After the pause, Moos returns to the machine, this time pushing and pulling the handle of the lever. Before long he succeeds in raising it through the 90-degree arc, whereupon he takes the chip from the holder and immediately uses it to get a grape from the vending machine. Thereafter, he readily reinstates the lever-pushing response, procuring his chips (and grapes) without difficulty.

Two aspects of this experiment are especially noteworthy. First, there was formed, in the second stage of the experiment, a clear-cut discrimination, in which the S^D was a white poker chip and the S^Δ was a brass one. In the presence of the former, Moos's manipulative response produced a grape; in the presence of the latter, it did not. Secondly, the white chip became a secondary reinforcer, alone sufficient to strengthen the lever-pushing response (even when, as shown in a later stage of the same experiment, the chips could not be exchanged for grapes until later). Thus, it appears that *a discriminative stimulus for one response may be the secondary reinforcer of another.*

Essentially the same experiment as the one with Moos has been carried out with rats, cats, dogs, and children, not to mention baby chicks, and the results have always been the same. It is now quite certain that if a stimulus is to become a secondary reinforcer it must become a *discriminative* stimulus. It is not enough to say that if a stimulus has merely been present on all occasions when a response is reinforced it will itself become reinforcing; the stimulus must have been *absent* on occasions when the response is *not* reinforced.

Maybe you can see now, better than before, how *chains* get formed. In Section 14, it was noted that a chain is no more than a string of S^D——R^D relations, but no direct mention was made of the part played in this by reinforcement. Now it should be apparent that the discriminative cue for a response that gets primary reinforcement becomes reinforcing to the response that *produces* this cue. In other words, every S^D in a chain becomes a secondary reinforcer for the response that produces it.

This means that, in a sense, chains are established in

a backward fashion—that the first link is the last one to be added to the series. Recall the behavior of Pliny, the rat. The first link in his chain, the string-pulling response, could not have been strengthened unless the marble had already become rewarding; manipulation of the marble, in carrying and lifting, could not have been strengthened unless the tube had not, in some way, become rewarding too; dropping the marble could not have been strengthened without the magazine sound; and finally, approach-to-tray behavior depended on the presence of the primary reinforcement, food.

Secondary reinforcers in the chain also explain why the first responses of the series get to be strong when the ultimate, primary reinforcer is so far away in time. Or, to say it in another way, they explain why primary reinforcement can be "delayed." Actually, the period of possible delay of a primary reinforcer is probably very short, a matter of seconds. If it appears to be longer, that is because a chain of responses, each with its own immediate, *secondary* reinforcement, fills the gap.

At this point, if we take S^r as our symbol of a secondary reinforcer, and S^R as our symbol of a primary reinforcer, a final diagram will serve to picture the state of affairs that now prevails.

$$
\begin{array}{llll}
S^\triangle & R^\triangle & S^\triangle & R^\triangle \\
S^D \!\!-\!\!-\!\!-\!\!-\!\!-\!\!-\!\!-\!\!-\!\!R^D \longrightarrow S^{rD}\!\!-\!\!-\!\!-\!\!-\!\!-\!\!-\!\!-\!\!-\!\!R^D \longrightarrow S^R \\
S^\triangle & R^\triangle & S^\triangle & R^\triangle
\end{array}
$$

Here we have, as the first link of a chain, a discriminative stimulus, giving rise to a differentiated response. This is followed by a secondary reinforcer that is, at the same time, the discriminative stimulus for the next differentiated response in the chain; and this leads, finally, to a primary reinforcer. The first S^D would, of course, be an S^r for any additional link that was added to the ones already connected.

The tremendous influence of secondary reinforcement in human affairs is seen most conspicuously in the case of those stimuli or stimulus compounds that have commonly been followed, at not too great a distance, by primary reinforcement. Most interesting, perhaps, are those compounds that are provided by the behavior of other persons. For example, from birth until death the "attentive" behavior of others is a common preliminary to such primary reinforcers as food, drink, and relief from discomfort. *Attention* therefore becomes, for most of us, an important secondary reward, and it may be the strengthener of a wide range of activities—all the way from the simple "Look at me, Daddy!" of early childhood to the recital of aches and pains that so often accompanies old age.

Approval, in the form of a smile, a nod, a "Yes," or their equivalent (different persons show approval in different ways), is another aspect of the behavior of others that is often the forerunner of more basic things. Although not so obvious a secondary reinforcer as attention, it still figures prominently in most of our social contacts. "Approval-seeking," when extreme, is frowned upon in our society, possibly even more than "attention-seeking," but there are few of us who do not seem to be rewarded by the "good will" of others at one time or another.

Affectionate behavior (kisses, caresses, embraces, and the like) on the part of others is also reinforcing to most of us, presumably because of its relation to several kinds of primary reinforcement, including the sexual and "maternal." The stimulus aspects of this behavior, like that of approval, show much variation between individuals and groups, and the pattern may be hard to distinguish from that of coquetry, or even submissiveness (see below). "Signs of affection," by which we mean the affectionate behavior itself, are not even exactly the same from person to person.

Many people in our society are reinforced by the "giving-in" of others, by "having one's own way." This *submission* or submissive behavior is even harder to pin down as a special stimulus pattern than is affection or approval, but anyone can think of numerous instances. "After you, sir!" "May we serve you, Madam?" "You can have my lollipop, Johnny." "This way, sir, we have a special table for you!" "You can be the pitcher, Bill." "That's O.K., it didn't hurt much!" These utterances derive their reinforcing power from the fact that they, or responses like them, have sometimes signaled more concrete rewards, or the removal of obstacles in one's path to such. They encourage the development of a dominant, self-assertive, or "masculine" style of life on the part of the person to whom they are directed.

Dominant persons, in turn, commonly grant favors to those who give them priorities. The one who steps aside for another may at least be thanked, or encouraged to follow along; the salesclerk is commended to the management for politeness; Bobby is given a chance to ride on Johnny's bicycle; the headwaiter is lavishly tipped; Bill may let George play first base; and the little man with the bruised foot may be left the evening paper at the next subway stop. All this encourages the adoption of a deferential, subservient, or "feminine" mode of reacting, and it may even result in a courting of dominance on the part of others. Unfortunately, the person whose reinforcers consist mainly of "leavings" may also become the prey of anxiety and fear.

Attention, approval, affection, submissiveness, and

dominance may be difficult to identify as stimuli for our behavior, but there is one class of secondary reinforcers that doesn't give much trouble. This is the class of "token rewards," an example of which was discussed a few pages ago, in the form of Moos's white poker chip. Money, of course, is the chief specimen here. Its reinforcing power in our society can hardly be overestimated. But there are others, somewhat less negotiable, that are easily singled out. They range all the way from gold stars, report cards, prizes, scholarship awards, and diplomas to loving cups, medals, citations, and newspaper accounts of our past achievements. They are usually not the immediate occasions for primary reinforcement, but they lead us down the road thereto!

These aren't the only classes of "generalized" * reinforcers that might have been mentioned here; and this is not as detailed an account as might have been offered. If, however, on looking back over the section, you can find that you have gone one step ahead in your understanding of human conduct, that will be enough. If you can see that secondary reinforcement is based on the establishment of a discrimination; and if you can see that Moos's poker chip is not hopelessly distant from the reward-value of "money, strength, age, title, rank, and position" (page 1) in human affairs, then there's no need to add more here.

* "Generalized" is the term sometimes applied to a secondary reinforcer the strength of which is derived from its connection with more than one kind of primary reinforcement.

16 *Secondary Negative Reinforcement*

Fifty-odd years ago, Vladimir Bekhterev, a Russian "reflexologist," described a method of conditioning that was, in his opinion, far superior to that employed by his rival, Ivan Pavlov. It could be used more readily with human subjects, and it involved motor rather than glandular behavior. It required only that a neutral stimulus (such as a tone) be paired with an electric shock to the foot or the hand, until the former came to produce the flexion or withdrawal movement that was the unconditioned response to the shock. The tone usually preceded the shock by a couple of seconds, and the shock did not follow the tone if the withdrawal response took place within that period.

John Watson adopted the technique in 1916, and it has been quite popular in American laboratories ever since, in both human and animal research. Only recently, however, have we recognized fully what was embodied within it. Watson thought, as Bekhterev and Pavlov had thought before him, that the procedure was the same, in all important respects, as that employed in conditioning the salivary response of dogs. Was there not a pairing of a neutral with an unconditioned stimulus? Did not the neutral stimulus eventually come to elicit the unconditioned response? To all appearances, the answer was Yes; but there were some disturbing considerations.

For one thing, the report came regularly from
several animal laboratories that the flexion or withdrawal response to the *conditioned* stimulus was
distinctly different from the response to the *unconditioned* stimulus, the shock, except for a little while
during the first stage of conditioning. Although the
responses were recognizably similar, the response to
shock was usually described as reflex-like (respondent),
whereas that to the tone or other conditioned stimulus
was said to resemble voluntary (operant) behavior. The
former was a quick, convulsive movement, involving
widespread muscular action; the latter was a smooth,
deliberate, and quite specific form of response.

A second bothersome fact was this. If a strictly Pavlovian procedure was employed—that is, if the neutral
stimulus was regularly followed by the shock except
on test occasions, a clear case of conditioning was very
difficult to demonstrate. Only when the response to the
conditioned stimulus succeeded in *avoiding* the on-
coming shock did there develop a specific motor response that was distinct from a diffuse, "sitting-tight"
sort of behavior.

The results of the human studies of foot-, hand-, or
finger-withdrawal conditioning were also puzzling. Subnormal children, in Bekhterev's laboratory, conditioned more readily than normal children; girls conditioned more readily than boys; younger children
conditioned more readily than older ones; and strong
shock was more effective than weak shock. The finding
with respect to shock intensity was confirmed in American laboratories with adult subjects, but even with
strong shock, some subjects failed to condition at all.
Often, the animal results were confirmed. Diffuse
responding was replaced by highly specific reactions as
conditioning progressed; the conditioned response was

evoked less quickly than the unconditioned; and conditioning was somewhat better when the avoidance of shock was possible. In addition, the human findings were noted to depend upon the kind of instructions given and the previous experience of the subjects in similar situations.

The key to many of these problems is to be found in what may be called, clumsily, "secondary negative reinforcement." You will remember the distinction, back in Section 5, between *positive* and *negative* reinforcement. Positive reinforcers were defined there as "all those stimuli that, when *presented,* act to *strengthen* the behavior that they follow." Negative reinforcers were defined as stimuli the *removal* of which is *strengthening,* or the *presentation* of which is *weakening.* Then, in Section 15, came the distinction between *primary* and *second*ary reinforcers. But the only secondary reinforcers described were of the positive sort. They were the stimuli which, through a special kind of association with positive reinforcers, became positively reinforcing themselves. No account whatever was taken of those stimuli which, through association with *negative* reinforcers, took on a similar negative function.

This neglect will now be remedied if you will consider another simple experiment upon that relatively simple organism, the laboratory white rat. This time, our apparatus is a two-roomed box, with a connecting door. The interior of one room is painted white, and the floor is a metal grid through the bars of which an electric shock can be delivered to the subject's feet. The other room is painted black, has a solid wooden floor, and is nearly light-proof. The ceiling of each room is a hinged lid that can be raised to put the animal into, or take him out of, the box. One wall of the white room is of glass, through which the animal may be observed by the experimenter.

The procedure on the first day of the experiment is simply that of placing the rat in the white room, with the shock turned on in the grid, and leaving him there until he jumps through the black-curtained open doorway into the dark room. As you might expect, he masters this little problem very quickly, within a matter of seconds. Whereupon the experimenter, after giving the rat a few minutes' rest, puts him through the experience again. And again, until a total of sixty runs from the white room to the black has been amassed. By this time, no one would question the statement that the shock was a negative reinforcer—that the jumping through the door was reinforced by the shock's removal. Nor would one doubt that the shock was an eliciting stimulus for "emotional" activity. And one might also conclude that the white room became, in the course of these runs, a *conditioned* stimulus for such activity.

The first test of such notions is made on the next day of the experiment. Again the subject is placed on the grid in the white room. Conditions are as before except for the fact that (*a*) no shock is delivered by the grid, and (*b*) the door behind the curtain is closed and locked. Within a fifteen-minute period of observation it becomes very apparent that the white room *does* act as a conditioned emotional stimulus. Urination, defecation, trembling, rapid breathing, and other classical indicators of fear are all to be seen in the rat's behavior. Even after four such quarter-hour periods of confinement within the white room, when some improvement can be noted, he still continues to cower and quiver in obvious distress.

A second test is made on the following day. Conditions are the same as on the second day, in that no shock is present in the white room, but the door to the dark room is now unlocked and open behind the separating curtain. The rat can now run to the dark room and remain there for a minute or so, after which he will be taken out, returned to the white room, and given another chance to escape. This is repeated for sixty test runs, or until he stops leaving the white room. Result: by the end of the day he is still leaping through the door with considerable speed, although not quite as rapidly as at first. The white room, in spite of the absence of shock within it, is still something to be run away from. Its "removal" is rewarding. By virtue of its earlier association with a negative reinforcer, the shock, it has become a negative reinforcer in its own right; it is now a *secondary* negative reinforcer.

Some further points ought to be made in connection with this experiment. One is that, if our animal had been confined for a long enough period in the white room on the second day, he would not have tried to leave it, except in an exploratory fashion, on the third. There would have been an extinction of the emotional response to the white-room stimuli (see Section 10). As a secondary negative reinforcer, this room would have lost its power, so that its removal would no longer have been rewarding. The rat would not have run away, simply because there was nothing to run away from.

A second point is that, if the rat had been given many more runs than sixty on the third day, his speed of running would have fallen off, ultimately to zero. The repeated placement of the animal within the white room on the third day would have had the same effect as a prolonged period of placement there on the second. The operant behavior of running would not have been extinguished; rather, its *cause* would have been removed as the white room lost its strength as a negative reinforcer or as a conditioned emotional stimulus.

A third point is this. Secondary negative reinforcement might have been demonstrated in this situation almost as easily if we had not permitted the rat to escape from the shock during the first day's training. We could have given him sixty brief shocks while confining him to the white room, and on the third day, we could have *taught* him to run through the door. Reinforcement, just as before, would have been the removal of the room where he was shocked.

Still another point. We could have conditioned our rat to remove something else than a white room. By altering the apparatus slightly, we could have conditioned him to jump from one room to the other to remove some special stimulus factor in the situation, say to turn off a light or the sound of a buzzer. Indeed, we could have shown that *any* kind of stimulation, not already negative, could be made so—even the stimulation produced by the animal's own movements. If a shock were to come on at five-second intervals unless our rat was standing on his hind legs, we would soon have an animal that spent most of his time with his forepaws in the air, thus escaping from his *other* ways of behavior, all of which were occasionally punished by the shock.

If now you will look again at the case of finger-, hand-, or foot-withdrawal conditioning, you may see it in a different light. It may now seem to be little more than avoidance behavior, like that displayed when a rat escapes from such a secondary negative reinforcer as a white room, a buzzer, or one of his own responses. If a dog lifts his right forefoot at the sound of a tone, and thus avoids an electric shock to his paw, his reinforcement may well be derived from the removal of some portion of the stimulus compound that has been paired with shock. We would not expect this operant lifting to resemble the respondent reaction to the shock any more than we would expect our rat's first mad scramble on the grid to resemble his later well-directed and unhurried passage through the door.

Results from the finger-withdrawal conditioning experiments do not parallel so closely those from the avoidance experiments. It may be, however, that human studies involve a *conflict* situation that is absent in the case of such organisms as dogs and rats. The behavior of some human subjects, including their reports of how they "feel," suggests a kind of competing avoidance. There is, on the one hand, a tendency to avoid the shock, which has been reinforced by the removal of a tone, a light, or some other threat. On the other hand, there is what you might call *an avoidance of an avoidance,* which has been reinforced originally because it gained social approval or eliminated disapproval. When a subject reports that he feels "silly" or "ashamed" to take his finger off the electrode when the signal comes for shock, it is strongly suggested that his past failures to "stand up under" such stimulation have been followed by an even more undesirable outcome; and that his actual failure to withdraw his finger (to avoid) is due to a countermovement that avoids it! Such an explanation as this does not at least run into opposition with the findings that finger-withdrawal is more readily developed with subnormal children than with normal, with girls than with boys, with younger children than with older, with strong shock than with weak, and so forth.

The role of secondary *positive* reinforcement in man's everyday life has already been given some attention in Section 15, and the importance of its control over our behavior has been emphasized. Secondary *negative* reinforcers are even more dramatically and vitally influential. A large percentage of our acts, both normal and abnormal, appear to get most of their strength from the removal of stimuli that have acquired aversive character. The most obvious are those responses that remove outside danger signals. Many games and most occupations require some degree of dodging, ducking, blocking, or warding-off behavior in response to environmental cues. Otherwise, as with the dog that fails to flex his leg at the sound of the tone, disaster may follow.

There are also activities that call for escape from cues provided by one's own movements. These are the activities in which balance and posture have an important role. Skiing, skating, bicycling, swimming, diving, and acrobatics of one sort or another are excellent examples. The bending, buckling, and sprawling movements of an amateur skier show vividly the way in which the cues from one movement lead to "correction" by another. Ultimately, the escapes from falling are made so quickly and subtly as to be unseen. In the turns and figures of the expert, there is little to suggest the clumsy avoidances (or the strains and bruises!) of the novice. And, to take a homelier example, the easy stride of the trained marcher contains no suggestion of the long series of half-falls and recoveries therefrom that were the chief ingredients of his "learning to walk."

A more serious aspect of this matter may be touched upon briefly in bringing this section to an end. Negative reinforcers, primary or secondary, make up a large share of what we call "punishment" (Section 10). In the primary case, there is actual bodily hurt, as when a child is spanked, slapped, or physically forced into submission. In the secondary case, it may be in the form of insult, mockery, jeers, or threats, among other things. In either case, however, an emotional response is conditioned, in Pavlovian fashion, and the situation becomes negatively reinforcing. Escape from the situation, or from any responses connected with it, is rewarding.

An obvious method of removing such a conditioned aversive situation is that taken by the white rat of our earlier example, who left the place of punishment as fast as he could. Human beings act like this on occasion. The place of emotional upset becomes, for them, a place never willingly to be reentered; they develop a "phobia" with respect to it and, through generalization, with respect to places that are like it. Sometimes, however, less obvious mechanisms of defense are used to keep from rearousing the signs or threats of punishment. A person may become unable to "see" or "hear" that which is negatively reinforcing; he may be unable to make the movement that earlier played a part in producing it; or he may develop behavior that keeps him preoccupied with alternative stimulation, itself negatively reinforcing, but to a lesser degree.

These and other modes of escape from the harassments of our present world are as interesting to the student of learning as they are to the one whose primary concern is with human maladjustment and its cure. The problems involved are not simple. Not nearly as simple as this rapid once-over of the field suggests. But we can see today, better than ever before, that they will require, for their full solution, a thorough understanding of the basic principles to which you have been introduced in this paper.

17   *Postscript*

In Section 1, page 3, some examples of learning were mentioned, and a few questions were raised about them. No definition of the concept was offered, and none was promised. Nor would one be very helpful now. It was hinted, however, that "learning" had come to include a large part of what today goes by the name of "psychology," and it was promised that your knowledge of the general principles treated in these pages would enable you to analyze many everyday instances of learning, including those mentioned at that time. So, now, it might be well for you to reread that first section, asking yourself if the promise has been kept, either wholly or in part. If it was, good! If it was not, and if you "applied yourself," then this little paper has fallen short of its goal. In which case the only remaining positive outcome would be an aroused interest in the further exploration of this field, or of psychology itself.

Appendix: Cumulative Response Curves and the Cumulative Recorder

Operant behavior, as noted at many points throughout this booklet, from Section 4 on, is measured primarily in terms of *frequency of occurrence*. If an act occurs often, we call it strong; if it seldom occurs, we call it weak. If a child is conditioned to press a lever for small pieces of candy, the frequency of pressing will increase rapidly as a result of the first few reinforcements of the response. Later on, as the candy loses its appeal, the frequency will gradually diminish. At first the response was strengthened; later, it became weak.

You can think of this also in terms of *rate of response*—responses per second, responses per minute, or responses per hour. In conditioning, the response rate increases, from almost zero responses per minute to as many as twenty or thirty. During satiation, as the candy continues to be eaten, the rate goes down gradually from this high value until it comes to a complete stop.

This is pictured graphically in Figures 1 and 2 below. Figure 1 shows how the rate of lever pressing (the number of presses per minute) may change during a three-minute period of conditioning. For the first thirty seconds or so in this graph, no responses were made. Then the responding began and, as the reinforcements came, the rate of pressing quickly climbed to a value of about twenty per minute. (You can check this by estimating the number of responses made between the two vertical dotted lines in the figure.) Since the rate *increases* throughout this record, the curve is said to show a *positive acceleration*.

Figure 1   *Figure 2*

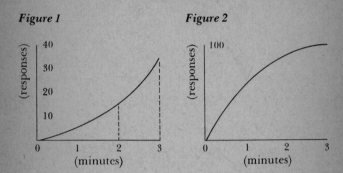

In Figure 2, more responses are represented. This graph shows that about 100 responses were emitted in a period of three minutes, at a gradually decreasing rate. You might think of this curve as a picture of a child's consumption of about 100 pieces of candy in a three-minute period of eating. Such a curve as this, showing a *decrease* in rate, is said to be *negatively accelerated*.

Figure 3 illustrates a special sort of curve, a straight-line curve. This is the sort of record you might get if candy were given, not for *every* pressing response, but only now and then—that is, intermittently. Three hundred responses were made here within a three-minute period, and they were made at the rate of 100 responses per minute. The little marks or "pips" along the line are put there to show when the reinforcements came—after about how many responses and how much time.

Figure 3

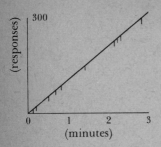

It would be very useful to have a machine that would automatically produce rate curves like these at the very time when the responses are being made. We would then be saved the trouble of counting up responses during successive units of time (say every minute) and making such plots as those shown in Figures 1, 2, and 3, sometimes long after the actual observations of behavior have been carried out. If the subject in the experiment (our little girl, for example) constructed her own graphical record as she went along, it would not only save us a lot of work later, it would tell us from moment to moment during the experiment just exactly what was going on in terms of the rate of response.

We do have such a machine! It is called a *cumulative recorder,* and it is one of the most useful of modern instruments in the experimental study of behavior. It produces just such curves as those we have considered, and many others. It does so by the simple *addition* (*cumulation*) of *responses* and *time* to the graphic record (the curve). Let's see how this takes place.

We begin with some response the rate of which we

want to record, as in the examples already mentioned.
Suppose the response is lever pressing. Every time that
the lever is pressed down far enough, an electric
switch is closed. When the switch closes, it activates the
mechanism which makes the recording pen move vertically a tiny step toward the top of a sheet of recording paper. If nothing else were happening, a series of
such responses would simply add up to a straight line
on the paper, from the bottom to the top, just like the
vertical line marked *Responses* in Figures 1, 2, or 3.

But something else does happen. At the moment we
start the machine so that we can get the response
record, the paper beneath the writing pen is pulled
very slowly and steadily *to the left,* at a speed of only
a few millimeters per minute. If this movement were
continued for some time, and if no responses were
made, the pen would appear to draw a line *to the
right,* just like the horizontal line of *Minutes* in each
of our three figures. (You can see how this works by
pulling a sheet of paper slowly to the left under a
pencil that you hold in a fixed position but pressing
lightly on the paper surface.) Responses alone would
make a vertical line; time alone would make a horizontal line.

When responses are made while time goes on, a
cumulative recorder will make curves like those of
our examples, or like combinations of such curves.
To get a detailed picture of how this might happen,
let us suppose that we have already drawn, on a sheet
of recording paper, a line for *Responses* and a line for
Minutes, as shown in Figure 4. Suppose, also, that we
have marked off points on each line at regular intervals to show the number of responses or the amount
of time it would take to get that far. Now let us place

the recording pen at zero, where the two lines meet, and start the machine. Imagine that, as time goes on, it is possible for some organism to depress a lever, get a reinforcement, and automatically record the response. Remember, each response will raise the pen one small step on the paper, and each minute of time will show itself as a short horizontal distance of pen travel to the right.

In Figure 4, it appears that the first response occurred after about six minutes of time, raising the pen one step above the base-line. After another three minutes of pen movement to the right, another response occurred and the pen moved up another step. The next two responses came at approximately two-minute intervals, and after that they came fairly steadily, at a rate of about one response per minute, until about fourteen responses had been made. Then,

Figure 4

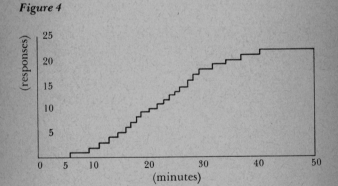

gradually, the time between responses gets longer and longer. Finally, all responding stops, and the time line continues, parallel with the base-line, until the end of the record. Our cumulative response curve has been constructed. We could now drop our marker back to the base-line and start another record.

If you could get rid of the step-like quality of this record, say by squinting at it or by viewing it from a distance, you could recognize that we have made a "curve" that is similar in some respects to those shown in Figures 1, 2, and 3. At first, there is a slight positive acceleration, something like that of Figure 1. Then there is a straight-line segment, like that of Figure 3, in which responses come at a fairly constant rate. And, finally, there is a negative acceleration, like that shown in Figure 2.

Although Figure 4 has its curve constructed in a special way, to show positive acceleration, negative acceleration, and a fairly constant rate of responding, the results are not much different from what might have been obtained in a real experiment. The record could represent, first, the conditioning of a lever-pressing response in a child, with sizable pieces of candy as reinforcements for each response; the second part could represent a steady period of responding-and-eating, after the response had been conditioned; and the final part of the curve could be taken as a picture of decreased responding due to satiation with the candy.

Two further points should be made before we leave this matter of the cumulative recorder and its operation. First, the step-like appearance of a cumulative response curve is not usually as obvious as it is in Figure 4. If the response units are very small and the time movement is very slow, it would be hard to see any steps at all; the curve would look almost as smooth as those in our first three figures. (We could, of course, exaggerate the step effect by making the pen move farther with each response and having faster movement in the time direction.)

Secondly, even with small steps and slow speeds, some organisms, such as pigeons, respond at such high rates that the marker would soon run off the top of the paper if nothing stopped it. For this reason, cumulative recorders are equipped with a reset mechanism that automatically drops the pen back to the base-line when it reaches a certain height on the recording paper (when a certain number of responses have been made). The effect is similar to that shown in Figure 4 at the end of the record. Long-term responding at a high rate might show many such drops and climbs. (This doesn't mean, of course, that we *subtract* responses from the number already made; cumulative curves, as the name suggests, *accumulate* responses—they only *add*. If we had all the room we needed on the recording paper, our record would keep on climbing to the end, without any need for starting over at the bottom.)

Suggested Readings

For the person who wants to go beyond this brief introduction to reinforcement theory and the problem of learning, the following books, to be read in the order of mention, are suggested.

Holland, James G., and B. F. Skinner. *The Analysis of Behavior*. New York: McGraw-Hill, 1961.

Ferster, C. B., and Mary Carol Perrott. *Behavior Principles*. New York: Appleton-Century-Crofts, 1968.

Skinner, B. F. *Science and Human Behavior*. New York: Macmillan, 1953.

Millenson, J. R. *Principles of Behavioral Analysis*. New York: Macmillan, 1967.

All these books are aimed at the beginning student of psychology, but they differ greatly in content, form, and readability. The Holland-Skinner text is *programmed*, the first of its kind in psychology. It is in some degree an abbreviated and simplified version of Skinner's *Science and Human Behavior*, to which it is a good introduction. The Ferster-Perrott book was written for use in a programmed *course*, but can be profitably read in a conventional manner. It was designed "to make the reader proficient in analyzing man's complex interaction with his natural environment" and goes far in relating laboratory findings and procedures to everyday life. *Science and Human Be-*

havior, written for the educated layman as well as the university student, is an impressive application of reinforcement thinking to the detailed analysis of individual and social behavior in our time. Millenson's *Principles of Behavioral Analysis* attempts to provide "a rigorous, data-oriented introduction to behavioral psychology" for university students in a one-year course that would ordinarily carry natural science credit.

Date Due

MAR 13 '78		
APR 17 '78		